THE ALASKA CONSTITUTION

University of Alaska Press, Fairbanks

Published by
University of Alaska Press
P.O. Box 756240
Fairbanks, AK 99775-6240

Cover and interior design by UA Press.

Article XIV: Apportionment Schedule (not included)
Repealed by 1998 Ballot Measure No. 3.
The Division of Elections publishes maps and district descriptions resulting from the Proclamation of Redistricting by the Alaska Redistricting Board, April 25, 2002.

Library of Congress Cataloging-in-Publication Data

Names: Alaska, enacting jurisdiction.
Title: The Alaska Constitution.
Other titles: Constitution
Description: Fairbanks : University of Alaska Press, 2020. | Summary: "The
    Alaska State Constitution, ratified by the people in 1956, became
    operative with the proclamation of statehood on January 3, 1959. The
    constitution was drafted by fifty-five delegates who convened at the
    University of Alaska to determine the authority vested in the state
    legislature, executive, judiciary, and other functions of government.
    This conveniently sized new edition will make the Alaska State
    Constitution accessible to all"-- Provided by publisher.
Identifiers: LCCN 2019042806 (print) | LCCN 2019042807 (ebook) | ISBN
    9781602234109 (paperback) | ISBN 9781602234116 (ebook)
Subjects: LCSH: Constitutional law--Alaska. | Constitutions--Alaska.
Classification: LCC KFA1601 1956 .A59 2020 (print) | LCC KFA1601 1956
    (ebook) | DDC 342.798--dc23
LC record available at https://lccn.loc.gov/2019042806
LC ebook record available at https://lccn.loc.gov/2019042807

PRINTED IN CANADA

*for all Alaskans working toward a
fair, balanced, and equitable state*

Table of Contents

Article I
Declaration of Rights

Inherent
Rights

Section 1. This constitution is dedicated to the principles that all persons have a natural right to life, liberty, the pursuit of happiness, and the enjoyment of the rewards of their own industry; that all persons are equal and entitled to equal rights, opportunities, and protection under the law; and that all persons have corresponding obligations to the people and to the State.

Source of
Government

Section 2. All political power is inherent in the people. All government originates with the people, is founded upon their will only, and is instituted solely for the good of the people as a whole.

Civil Rights

Section 3. No person is to be denied the enjoyment of any civil or political right because of race, color, creed, sex, or national origin. The legislature shall implement this section. [Amended 1972]

Freedom of
Religion

Section 4. No law shall be made respecting an establishment of religion, or prohibiting the free exercise thereof.

Freedom of
Speech

Section 5. Every person may freely speak, write, and publish on all subjects, being responsible for the abuse of that right.

Assembly;
Petition

Section 6. The right of the people peaceably to assemble, and to petition the government shall never be abridged.

Due Process

Section 7. No person shall be deprived of life, liberty, or property, without due process of law. The right of all persons to fair and just treatment in the course of legislative and executive investigations shall not be infringed.

Grand Jury

Section 8. No person shall be held to answer for a capital, or otherwise infamous crime, unless on a presentment or indictment of a grand jury, except in cases arising in the armed forces in time of war or public danger. Indictment may be waived by the accused. In that case the prosecution shall be by in formation. The grand jury shall consist of at least twelve citizens, a majority of whom concurring may return an indictment. The power of grand juries to investigate and make recommendations concerning the public welfare or safety shall never be suspended.

Jeopardy and Self-incrimination

Section 9. No person shall be put in jeopardy twice for the same offense. No person shall be compelled in any criminal proceeding to be a witness against himself.

Treason

Section 10. Treason against the State consists only in levying war against it, or in adhering to its enemies, giving them aid and comfort. No person shall be convicted of treason, unless on the testimony of two witnesses to the same overt act, or on confession in open court.

Rights of Accused

Section 11. In all criminal prosecutions, the accused shall have the right to a speedy and public trial, by an impartial jury of twelve, except that the legislature may provide for a jury of not more than twelve nor less than six in courts not of record. The accused is entitled to be informed of the nature and cause of the accusation; to be released on bail, except for capital offenses when the proof is evident or the presumption great; to be confronted with the witnesses against him; to have compulsory process for obtaining wit nesses in his favor, and to have the assistance of counsel for his defense.

Criminal
Administration

Section 12. Excessive bail shall not be required, nor excessive fines imposed, nor cruel and unusual punishments inflicted. Criminal administration shall be based upon the following: the need for protecting the public, community condemnation of the offender, the rights of victims of crimes, restitution from the offender, and the principle of reformation. [Amended 1994]

Habeas
Corpus

Section 13. The privilege of the writ of habeas corpus shall not be suspended, unless when in cases of rebellion or actual or imminent invasion, the public safety requires it.

Searches and
Seizures

Section 14. The right of the people to be secure in their persons, houses and other property, papers, and effects, against unreasonable searches and seizures, shall not be violated. No warrants shall issue, but upon probable cause, supported by oath or affirmation, and particularly describing the place to be searched, and the persons or things to be seized.

Prohibited
State Action

Section 15. No bill of attainder or ex post facto law shall be passed. No law impairing the obligation of contracts, and no law making any irrevocable grant of special privileges or immunities shall be passed. No conviction shall work corruption of blood or forfeiture of estate.

**Civil Suits;
Trial by Jury**

Section 16. In civil cases where the amount in controversy exceeds two hundred fifty dollars, the right of trial by a jury of twelve is preserved to the same extent as it existed at common law. The legislature may make provision for a verdict by not less than three-fourths of the jury and, in courts not of record, may provide for a jury of not less than six or more than twelve.

**Imprisonment
for Debt**

Section 17. There shall be no imprisonment for debt. This section does not prohibit civil arrest of absconding debtors.

**Eminent
Domain**

Section 18. Private property shall not be taken or damaged for public use without just compensation.

**Right to
Bear Arms**

Section 19. A well-regulated militia being necessary to the security of a free state, the right of the people to keep and bear arms shall not be infringed. The individual right to keep and bear arms shall not be denied or infringed by the State or a political subdivision of the State. [Amended 1994]

**Quartering
Soldiers**

Section 20. No member of the armed forces shall in time of peace be quartered in any house with out the consent of the owner or occupant, or in time of war except as prescribed by law. The military shall be in strict subordination to the civil power.

Construction

Section 21. The enumeration of rights in this constitution shall not impair or deny others retained by the people.

**Right of
Privacy**

Section 22. The right of the people to privacy is recognized and shall not be infringed. The legislature shall implement this section. [Amended 1972]

Resident
Preference

Section 23. This constitution does not prohibit the State from granting preferences, on the basis of Alaska residence, to residents of the State over nonresidents to the extent permitted by the Constitution of the United States. [Amended 1988]

Rights of
Crime Victims

Section 24. Crime victims, as defined by law, shall have the following rights as provided by law: the right to be reasonably protected from the accused through the imposition of appropriate bail or conditions of release by the court; the right to confer with the prosecution; the right to be treated with dignity, respect, and fairness during all phases of the criminal and juvenile justice process; the right to timely disposition of the case following the arrest of the accused; the right to obtain information about and be allowed to be present at all criminal or juvenile proceedings where the accused has the right to be present; the right to be allowed to be heard, upon request, at sentencing, before or after conviction or juvenile adjudication, and at any proceeding where the accused's release from custody is considered; the right to restitution from the accused; and the right to be informed, upon request, of the accused's escape or release from custody before or after conviction or juvenile adjudication. [Amended 1994]

Marriage

Section 25. To be valid or recognized in this State, a marriage may exist only between one man and one woman. [Amended 1998]

Article II
The Legislature

Legislative
Power;
Membership

Section 1. The legislative power of the State is vested in a legislature consisting of a senate with a membership of twenty and a house of representatives with a membership of forty.

Members:
Qualifications

Section 2. A member of the legislature shall be a qualified voter who has been a resident of Alaska for at least three years and of the district from which elected for at least one year, immediately preceding his filing for office. A senator shall be at least twenty five years of age and a representative at least twenty-one years of age.

Election and
Terms

Section 3. Legislators shall be elected at general elections. Their terms begin on the fourth Monday of the January following election unless otherwise provided by law. The term of representatives shall be two years, and the term of senators, four years. One-half of the senators shall be elected every two years.

Vacancies

Section 4. A vacancy in the legislature shall be filled for the unexpired term as provided by law. If no provision is made, the governor shall fill the vacancy by appointment.

Dis-
qualifications

Section 5. No legislator may hold any other office or position of profit under the United States or the State. During the term for which elected and for one year thereafter, no legislator may be nominated, elected, or appointed to any other office or position of profit which has been created, or the salary or emoluments of which have been increased, while he was a member. This section shall not prevent any person from seeking or holding the office of governor, secretary of state, or member of Congress. This section shall not apply to employment by or election to a constitutional convention.

Immunities

Section 6. Legislators may not be held to answer before any other tribunal for any statement made in the exercise of their legislative duties while the legislature is in session. Members attending, going to, or returning from legislative sessions are not subject to civil process and are privileged from a rest except for felony or breach of the peace.

Salary and
Expenses

Section 7. Legislators shall receive annual salaries. They may receive a per diem allowance for expenses while in session and are entitled to travel expenses going to and from sessions. Presiding officers may receive additional compensation.

Regular
Sessions

Section 8. The legislature shall convene in regular session each year on the fourth Monday in January, but the month and day may be changed by law. The legislature shall adjourn from regular session no later than one hundred twenty consecutive calendar days from the date it convenes except that a regular session may be extended once for up to ten consecutive calendar days. An extension of the regular session requires the affirmative vote of at least two-thirds of the membership of each house of the legislature. The legislature shall adopt as part of the uniform rules of procedure deadlines for scheduling session work not inconsistent with provisions controlling the length of the session. [Amended 1984]

Special
Sessions

Section 9. Special sessions may be called by the governor or by vote of two-thirds of the legislators. The vote may be conducted by the legislative council or as prescribed by law. At special sessions called by the governor, legislation shall be limited to subjects designated in his proclamation calling the session, to subjects presented by him, and the reconsideration of bills vetoed by him after adjournment of the last regular session. Special sessions are limited to thirty days. [Amended 1976]

Adjournment

Section 10. Neither house may adjourn or recess for longer than three days unless the other con curs. If the two houses cannot agree on the time of adjournment and either house certifies the disagreement to the governor, he may adjourn the legislature.

Interim
Committees

Section 11. There shall be a legislative council, and the legislature may establish other interim committees. The council and other interim committees may meet between legislative sessions. They may perform duties and employ personnel as provided by the legislature. Their members may receive an allowance for expenses while performing their duties.

Rules

Section 12. The houses of each legislature shall adopt uniform rules of procedure. Each house may choose its officers and employees. Each is the judge of the election and qualifications of its members and may expel a member with the concurrence of two-thirds of its members. Each shall keep a journal of its proceedings. A majority of the membership of each house constitutes a quorum to do business, but a smaller number may adjourn from day to day and may compel attendance of absent members. The legislature shall regulate lobbying.

Form of Bills

Section 13. Every bill shall be confined to one subject unless it is an appropriation bill or one codifying, revising, or rearranging existing laws. Bills for appropriations shall be confined to appropriations. The subject of each bill shall be expressed in the title. The enacting clause shall be: "Be it enacted by the Legislature of the State of Alaska."

Passage of Bills

Section 14. The legislature shall establish the procedure for enactment of bills into law. No bill may become law unless it has passed three readings in each house on three separate days, except that any bill may be advanced from second to third reading on the same day by concurrence of three-fourths of the house considering it. No bill may become law without an affirmative vote of a majority of the membership of each house. The yeas and nays on final passage shall be entered in the journal.

Veto   **Section 15.** The governor may veto bills passed by the legislature. He may, by veto, strike or reduce items in appropriation bills. He shall return any vetoed bill, with a statement of his objections, to the house of origin.

Action Upon Veto   **Section 16.** Upon receipt of a veto message during a regular session of the legislature, the legislature shall meet immediately in joint session and reconsider passage of the vetoed bill or item. Bills to raise revenue and appropriation bills or items, although vetoed, become law by affirmative vote of three-fourths of the membership of the legislature. Other vetoed bills become law by affirmative vote of two-thirds of the membership of the legislature. Bills vetoed after adjournment of the first regular session of the legislature shall be reconsidered by the legislature sitting as one body no later than the fifth day of the next regular or special session of that legislature. Bills vetoed after adjournment of the second regular session shall be reconsidered by the legislature sitting as one body no later than the fifth day of a special session of that legislature, if one is called. The vote on reconsideration of a vetoed bill shall be entered on the journals of both houses. [Amended 1976]

Bills Not Signed   **Section 17.** A bill becomes law if, while the legislature is in session, the governor neither signs nor vetoes it within fifteen days, Sundays excepted, after its delivery to him. If the legislature is not in session and the governor neither signs nor vetoes a bill within twenty days, Sundays excepted, after its delivery to him, the bill becomes law.

Effective Date **Section 18.** Laws passed by the legislature be come effective ninety days after, enactment. The legislature may, by concurrence of two-thirds of the membership of each house, provide for another effective date.

Local or Special Acts **Section 19.** The legislature shall pass no local or special act if a general act can be made applicable. Whether a general act can be made applicable shall be subject to judicial determination. Local acts necessitating appropriations by a political subdivision may not become effective unless approved by a majority of the qualified voters voting thereon in the subdivision affected.

Impeachment **Section 20.** All civil officers of the State are subject to impeachment by the legislature. Impeachment shall originate in the senate and must be approved by a two-thirds vote of its members. The motion for impeachment shall list fully the basis for the proceeding. Trial on impeachment shall be con ducted by the house of representatives. A supreme court justice designated by the court shall preside at the trial. Concurrence of two-thirds of the members of the house is required for a judgment of impeachment. The judgment may not extend beyond removal from office, but shall not prevent proceedings in the courts on the same or related charges.

Suits Against the State **Section 21.** The legislature shall establish procedures for suits against the State.

Article III
The Executive

Executive
Power

Section 1. The executive power of the State is vested in the governor.

Governor:
Qualifications

Section 2. The governor shall be at least thirty years of age and a qualified voter of the State. He shall have been a resident of Alaska at least seven years immediately preceding his filing for office, and he shall have been a citizen of the United States for at least seven years.

Election

Section 3. The governor shall be chosen by the qualified voters of the State at a general election. The candidate receiving the greatest number of votes shall be governor.

Term
of Office

Section 4. The term of office of the governor is four years, beginning at noon on the first Monday in December following his election and ending at noon on the first Monday in December four years later.

Limit
on Tenure

Section 5. No person who has been elected governor for two full successive terms shall be again eligible to hold that office until one full term has intervened.

Dual Office
Holding

Section 6. The governor shall not hold any other office or position of profit under the United States, the State, or its political subdivisions.

Lieutenant
Governor
Duties

Section 7. There shall be a lieutenant governor. He shall have the same qualifications as the governor and serve for the same term. He shall perform such duties as may be prescribed by law and as may be delegated to him by the governor. [Amended 1970]

Election

Section 8. The lieutenant governor shall be nominated in the manner provided by law for nominating candidates for other elective offices. In the general election the votes cast for a candidate for governor shall be considered as cast also for the candidate for lieutenant governor running jointly with him. The candidate whose name appears on the ballot jointly with that of the successful candidate for governor shall be elected lieutenant governor. [Amended 1970]

Acting
Governor

Section 9. In case of the temporary absence of the governor from office, the lieutenant governor shall serve as acting governor. [Amended 1970]

Succession:
Failure to
Qualify

Section 10. If the governor-elect dies, resigns, or is disqualified, the lieutenant governor elected with him shall succeed to the office of governor for the full term. If the governor-elect fails to assume office for any other reason, the lieutenant governor elected with him shall serve as acting governor, and shall succeed to the office if the governor-elect does not assume his office within six months of the beginning of the term. [Amended 1970]

Vacancy

Section 11. In case of a vacancy in the office of governor for any reason, the lieutenant governor shall succeed to the office for the remainder of the term. [Amended 1970]

Absence

Section 12. Whenever for a period of six months, a governor has been continuously absent from office or has been unable to discharge the duties of his office by reason of mental or physical disability, the office shall be deemed vacant. The procedure for determining absence and disability shall be prescribed by law.

Further Succession

Section 13. Provision shall be made by law for succession to the office of governor and for an acting governor in the event that the lieutenant governor is unable to succeed to the office or act as governor. No election of a lieutenant governor shall be held except at the time of electing a governor. [Amended 1970]

Title and Authority

Section 14. When the lieutenant governor succeeds to the office of governor, he shall have the title, powers, duties and emoluments of that office. [Amended 1970]

Compensation

Section 15. The compensation of the governor and the lieutenant governor shall be prescribed by law and shall not be diminished during their term of office, unless by general law applying to all salaried officers of the State. [Amended 1970]

Governor: Authority

Section 16. The governor shall be responsible for the faithful execution of the laws. He may, by appropriate court action or proceeding brought in the name of the State, enforce compliance with any constitutional or legislative mandate, or restrain violation of any constitutional or legislative power, duty, or right by any officer, department, or agency of the State or any of its political subdivisions. This authority shall not be construed to authorize any action or proceeding against the legislature.

Convening Legislature

Section 17. Whenever the governor considers it in the public interest, he may convene the legislature, either house, or the two houses in joint session.

Messages to
Legislature

Section 18. The governor shall, at the beginning of each session, and may at other times, give the legislature information concerning the affairs of the State and recommend the measures he considers necessary.

Military
Authority

Section 19. The governor is commander-in-chief of the armed forces of the State. He may call out these forces to execute the laws, suppress or prevent insurrection or lawless violence, or repel invasion. The governor, as provided by law, shall appoint all general and flag officers of the armed forces of the State, subject to confirmation by a majority of the members of the legislature in joint session. He shall appoint and commission all other officers.

Martial Law

Section 20. The governor may proclaim martial law when the public safety requires it in case of rebellion or actual or imminent invasion. Martial law shall not continue for longer than twenty days without the approval of a majority of the members of the legislature in joint session.

Executive
Clemency

Section 21. Subject to procedure prescribed by law, the governor may grant pardons, commutations, and reprieves, and may suspend and remit fines and forfeitures. This power shall not extend to impeachment. A parole system shall be provided by law.

Executive Branch

Section 22. All executive and administrative offices, departments, and agencies of the state government and their respective functions, powers, and duties shall be allocated by law among and within not more than twenty principal departments, so as to group them as far as practicable according to major purposes. Regulatory, quasi-judicial, and temporary agencies may be established by law and need not be allocated within a principal department.

Reorganization

Section 23. The governor may make changes in the organization of the executive branch or in the assignment of functions among its units which he considers necessary for efficient administration. Where these changes require the force of law, they shall be set forth in executive orders. The legislature shall have sixty days of a regular session, or a full session if of shorter duration, to disapprove these executive orders. Unless disapproved by resolution concurred in by a majority of the members in joint session, these orders become effective at a date thereafter to be designated by the governor.

Supervision

Section 24. Each principal department shall be under the supervision of the governor.

Department Heads

Section 25. The head of each principal department shall be a single executive unless otherwise provided by law. He shall be appointed by the governor, subject to confirmation by a majority of the members of the legislature in joint session, and shall serve at the pleasure of the governor, except as otherwise provided in this article with respect to the secretary of state. The heads of all principal departments shall be citizens of the United States.

<table>
<tr><td>Boards and
Commissions</td><td>

Section 26. When a board or commission is at the head of a principal department or a regulatory or quasi-judicial agency, its members shall be appointed by the governor, subject to confirmation by a majority of the members of the legislature in joint session, and may be removed as provided by law. They shall b citizens of the United States. The board or commission may appoint a principal executive officer when authorized by law, but the appointment shall be subject to the approval of the governor.

</td></tr>
<tr><td>Recess
Appointments</td><td>

Section 27. The governor may make appoint ments to fill vacancies occurring during a recess of the legislature, in offices requiring confirmation by the legislature. The duration of such appointments shall be prescribed by law.

</td></tr>
</table>

Judicial Power and Jurisdiction

Section 1. The judicial power of the State is vested in a supreme court, a superior court, and the courts established by the legislature. The jurisdiction of courts shall be prescribed by law. The courts shall constitute a unified judicial system for operation and administration. Judicial districts shall be established by law.

Supreme Court

Section 2. (a) The supreme court shall be the highest court of the State, with final appellate jurisdiction. It shall consist of three justices, one of whom is chief justice. The number of justices may be increased by law upon the request of the supreme court.

(b) The chief justice shall be selected from among the justices of the supreme court by a majority vote of the justices. His term of office as chief justice is three years. A justice may serve more than one term as chief justice but he may not serve consecutive terms in that office. [Amended 1970]

Superior Court

Section 3. The superior court shall be the trial court of general jurisdiction and shall consist of five judges. The number of judges may be changed by law.

Qualifications of Justices and Judges

Section 4. Supreme court justices and superior court judges shall be citizens of the United States and of the State, licensed to practice law in the State, and possessing any additional qualifications prescribed by law. Judges of other courts shall be selected in a manner, for terms, and with qualifications prescribed by law.

Nomination and
Appointment

Section 5. The governor shall fill any vacancy in an office of supreme court justice or superior court judge by appointing one of two or more persons nominated by the judicial council.

Approval or
Rejection

Section 6. Each supreme court justice and superior court judge shall, in the manner provided by law, be subject to approval or rejection on a nonpartisan ballot at the first general election held more than three years after his appointment. Thereafter, each supreme court justice shall be subject to approval or rejection in a like manner every tenth year, and each superior court judge, every sixth year.

Vacancy

Section 7. The office of any supreme court justice or superior court judge becomes vacant ninety days after the election at which he is rejected by a majority of those voting on the question, or for which he fails to file his declaration of candidacy to succeed himself.

Judicial
Council

Section 8. The judicial council shall consist of seven members. Three attorney members shall be appointed for six-year terms by the governing body of the organized state bar. Three non-attorney members shall be appointed for six-year terms by the governor subject to confirmation by a majority of the members of the legislature in joint session. Vacancies shall be filled for the unexpired term in like manner. Appointments shall be made with due consideration to area representation and without regard to political affiliation. The chief justice of the supreme court shall be ex officio the seventh member and chairman of the judicial council. No member of the judicial council, except the chief justice, may hold any other office or

Judicial
Council
(cont.)

position of profit under the United States or the State. The judicial council shall act by concurrence of four or more members and according to rules which it adopts.

Additional
Duties

Section 9. The judicial council shall conduct studies for improvement of the administration of justice, and make reports and recommendations to the supreme court and to the legislature at intervals of not more than two years. The judicial council shall perform other duties assigned by law.

Commission
on Judicial Con-
duct

Section 10. The Commission on Judicial Conduct shall consist of nine members, as follows: three persons who are justices or judges of state courts, elected by the justices and judges of state courts; three members who have practiced law in this state for ten years, appointed by the governor from nominations made by the governing body of the organized bar and subject to confirmation by a majority of the members of the legislature in joint session; and three persons who are not judges, retired judges, or members of the state bar, appointed by the governor and subject to confirmation by a majority of the members of the legislature in joint session. In addition to being subject to impeachment under section 12 of this article, a justice or judge may be disqualified from acting as such and may be suspended, removed from office, retired, or censured by the supreme court upon the recommendation of the commission. The powers and duties of the commission and the bases for judicial disqualification shall be established by law. [Amended 1968 & 1982]

Retirement

Section 11. Justices and judges shall be retired at the age of seventy except as provided in this article. The basis and amount of retirement pay shall be prescribed by law. Retired judges shall render no further service on the bench except for special assignments as provided by court rule.

Impeachment

Section 12. Impeachment of any justice or judge for malfeasance or misfeasance in the performance of his official duties shall be according to procedure prescribed for civil officers.

Compensation

Section 13. Justices, judges, and members of the judicial council and the Commission on Judicial Qualifications shall receive compensation as prescribed by law. Compensation of justices and judges shall not be diminished during their terms of office, unless by general law applying to all salaried officers of the State. [Amended 1968]

Restrictions

Section 14. Supreme court justices and superior court judges while holding office may not practice law, hold office in a political party, or hold any other office or position of profit under the United States, the State, or its political subdivisions. Any supreme court justice or superior court judge filing for another elective public office forfeits his judicial position.

Rule-making Power

Section 15. The supreme court shall make and promulgate rules governing the administration of all courts. It shall make and promulgate rules governing practice and procedure in civil and criminal cases in all courts. These rules may be changed by the legislature by two-thirds vote of the members elected to each house.

Court
Administrtion

Section 16. The chief justice of the supreme court shall
be the administrative head of all courts. He may assign
judges from one court or division thereof to another
for temporary service. The chief justice shall, with the
approval of the supreme court, appoint an administrative
director to serve at the pleasure of the supreme court and
to supervise the administrative operations of the judicial
system. [Amended 1970]

Article V
Suffrage and Elections

Qualified
Voters

Section 1. Every citizen of the United States who is at least eighteen years of age, who meets registration residency requirements which may be prescribed by law, and who is qualified to vote under this article, may vote in any state or local election. A voter shall have been, immediately preceding the election, a thirty day resident of the election district in which he seeks to vote, except that for purposes of voting for President and Vice President of the United States other residency requirements may be prescribed by law. Additional voting qualifications may be prescribed by law for bond issue elections of political subdivisions. [Amended 1966, 1970 & 1972]

Dis-
qualifications

Section 2. No person may vote who has been convicted of a felony involving moral turpitude unless his civil rights have been restored. No person may vote who has been judicially determined to be of unsound mind unless the disability has been removed.

Methods of
Voting:
Election
Contests

Section 3. Methods of voting, including absentee voting, shall be prescribed by law. Secrecy of voting shall be preserved. The procedure for deter mining election contests, with right of appeal to the courts, shall be prescribed by law.

Voting
Precincts:
Registration

Section 4. The legislature may provide a system of permanent registration of voters, and may establish voting precincts within election districts.

General
Elections

Section 5. General elections shall be held on the second Tuesday in October of every even-numbered year, but the month and day may be changed by law.

Article VI
Legislative Apportionment

Houes
Districts

Section 1. Members of the house of representatives shall be elected by the qualified voters of the respective house districts. The boundaries of the house districts shall be set under this article following the official reporting of each decennial census of the United States. [Amended 1998]

Senate
Districts

Section 2. Members of the senate shall be elected by the qualified voters of the respective senate districts. The boundaries of the senate districts shall be set under this article following the official reporting of each decennial census of the United States. [Amended 1998]

Reapportion-
ment of House

Section 3. The Redistricting Board shall reapportion the house of representatives and the senate immediately following the official reporting of each decennial census of the United States. Reapportionment shall be based upon the population within each house and senate district as reported by the official decennial census of the United States. [Amended 1998]

Method of
Redistricting

Section 4. The Redistricting Board shall establish forty house districts, with each house district to elect one member of the house of representatives. The board shall establish twenty senate districts, each composed of two house districts, with each senate district to elect one senator. [Amended 1998]

Combining
Distrcits

Section 5. Should the total civilian population
within any election district fall below one-half
of the quotient, the district shall be attached to
an election district within its senate district, and
the reapportionment for the new district shall be
determined as provided in Section 4 of this article.
[Repealed by 1998 Ballot Measure No. 3]

District
Boundaries

Section 6. The Redistricting Board shall establish
the size and area of house districts, subject to the
limitations of this article. Each house district shall
be formed of contiguous and compact territory
containing as nearly as practicable a relatively
integrated socio-economic area. Each shall contain
a population as near as practicable to the quotient
obtained by dividing the population of the state by
forty. Each senate district shall be composed as near
as practicable of two contiguous house districts.
Consideration may be given to local government
boundaries. Drainage and other geographic features
shall be used in describing boundaries wherever
possible.

Modification
of Senate
Districts

Section 7. The senate districts, described in Section 2
of Article XIV, may be modified to reflect changes in
election districts. A district, although modified, shall
retain its total number of senators and its approximate
perimeter. [Repealed by 1998 Ballot Measure No. 3]

Redistricting
Board

Section 8. (a) There shall be a redistricting board. It shall consist of five members, all of whom shall be residents of the state for at least one year and none of whom may be public employees or officials at the time of or during the tenure of appointment. Appointments shall be made without regard to political affiliation. Board members shall be compensated.

(b) Members of the Redistricting Board shall be appointed in the year in which an official decennial census of the United States is taken and by September 1 of that year. The governor shall appoint two members of the board. The presiding officer of the senate, the presiding officer of the house of representatives, and the chief justice of the supreme court shall each appoint one member of the board. The appointments to the board shall be made in the order listed in this subsection. At least one board member shall be a resident of each judicial district that existed on January 1, 1999. Board members serve until a final plan for redistricting and proclamation of redistricting has been adopted and all challenges to it brought under section 11 of this article have been resolved after final remand or affirmation.(c) A person who was a member of the Redistricting Board at any time during the process leading to final adoption of a redistricting plan under section 10 of this article may not be a candidate for the legislature in the general election following the adoption of the final redistricting plan. [Amended 1998]

Board Actions

Section 9. The board shall elect one of its members chairman and may employ temporary assistants. Concurrence of three members of the Redistricting Board is required for actions of the Board, but a lesser number may conduct hearings. The board shall employ or contract for services of independent legal counsel. [Amended 1998]

Redistricting Plan and Proclamation

Section 10. (a) Within thirty days after the official reporting of the decennial census of the United States or thirty days after being duly appointed, whichever occurs last, the board shall adopt one or more proposed redistricting plans. The board shall hold public hearings on the proposed plan, or, if no single proposed plan is agreed on, on all plans proposed by the board. No later than ninety days after the board has been appointed and the official reporting of the decennial census of the United States, the board shall adopt a final redistricting plan and issue a proclamation of redistricting. The final plan shall set out boundaries of house and senate districts and shall be effective for the election of members of the legislature until after the official reporting of the next decennial census of the United States.

(b) Adoption of a final redistricting plan shall require the affirmative votes of three members of the Redistricting Board. [Amended 1998]

Enforcement

Section 11. Any qualified voter may apply to the superior court to compel the Redistricting Board, by mandamus or otherwise, to perform its duties under this article or to correct any error in redistricting. Application to compel the board to perform must be filed not later than thirty days following the expiration of the ninety-day period specified in this article. Application to compel correction of any error in redistricting must be filed within thirty days following the adoption of the final redistricting plan and proclamation by the board. Original jurisdiction in these matters is vested in the superior court. On appeal from the superior court, the cause shall be reviewed by the supreme court on the law and the facts. Notwithstanding section 15 of article IV, all dispositions by the superior court and the supreme court under this section shall be expedited and shall have priority over all other matters pending before the respective court. Upon a final judicial decision that a plan is invalid, the matter shall be returned to the board for correction and development of a new plan. If that new plan is declared invalid, the matter may be referred again to the board. [Amended 1998]

[The Division of Elections publishes maps and district descriptions resulting from the Proclamation of Redistricting by the Alaska Redistricting Board, April 25, 2002.]

Article VII
Health, Education, and Welfare

Public
Education

Section 1. The legislature shall by general law establish and maintain a system of public schools open to all children of the State, and may provide for other public educational institutions. Schools and institutions so established shall be free from sectarian control. No money shall be paid from public funds for the direct benefit of any religious or other private educational institution.

State
University

Section 2. The University of Alaska is hereby established as the state university and constituted a body corporate. It shall have title to all real and personal property now or hereafter set aside for or conveyed to it. Its property shall be administered and disposed of according to law.

Board of
Regents

Section 3. The University of Alaska shall be governed by a board of regents. The regents shall be appointed by the governor, subject to confirmation by a majority of the members of the legislature in joint session. The board shall, in accordance with law, formulate policy and appoint the president of the university. He shall be the executive officer of the board.

Public
Health

Section 4. The legislature shall provide for the promotion and protection of public health.

Public
Welfare

Section 5. The legislature shall provide for public welfare.

Article VIII
Natural Resources

Statement of Policy	**Section 1.** It is the policy of the State to encourage the settlement of its land and the development of its resources by making them available for maximum use consistent with the public interest.
General Authority	**Section 2.** The legislature shall provide for the utilization, development, and conservation of all natural resources belonging to the State, including land and waters, for the maximum benefit of its people.
Common Use	**Section 3.** Wherever occurring in their natural state, fish, wildlife, and waters are reserved to the people for common use.
Sustained Yield	**Section 4.** Fish, forests, wildlife, grasslands, and all other replenishable resources belonging to the State shall be utilized, developed, and maintained on the sustained yield principle, subject to preferences among beneficial uses.
Facilities and Improvements	**Section 5.** The legislature may provide for facilities, improvements, and services to assure greater utilization, development, reclamation, and settlement of lands, and to assure fuller utilization and development of the fisheries, wildlife, and waters.
State Public Domain	**Section 6.** Lands and interests therein, including submerged and tidal lands, possessed or acquired by the State, and not used or intended exclusively for governmental purposes, constitute the state public domain. The legislature shall provide for the selection of lands granted to the State by the United States, and for the administration of the state public domain.

Special
Purpose
Sites

Section 7. The legislature may provide for the acquisition of sites, objects, and areas of natural beauty or of historic, cultural, recreational, or scientific value. It may reserve them from the public domain and provide for their administration and preservation for the use, enjoyment, and welfare of the people.

Leases

Section 8. The legislature may provide for the leasing of, and the issuance of permits for exploration of, any part of the public domain or interest therein, subject to reasonable concurrent uses. Leases and permits shall provide, among other conditions, for payment by the party at fault for damage or in jury arising from noncompliance with terms governing concurrent use, and for forfeiture in the event of breach of conditions.

Sales and
Grants

Section 9. Subject to the provisions of this section, the legislature may provide for the sale or grant of state lands, or interests therein, and establish sales procedures. All sales or grants shall contain such reservations to the State of all resources as may be required by Congress or the State and shall provide for access to these resources. Reservation of access shall not unnecessarily impair the owners' use, prevent the control of trespass, or preclude compensation for damage.

Public
Notice

Section 10. No disposals or leases of state lands, or interests therein, shall be made without prior public notice and other safeguards of the public interest as may be prescribed by law.

Mineral
Rights

Section 11. Discovery and appropriation shall be the basis for establishing a right in those minerals reserved to the State which, upon the date of ratification of this constitution by the people of Alaska, were subject to location under the federal mining laws. Prior discovery, location, and filing, as pre scribed by law, shall establish a prior right to these minerals and also a prior right to permits, leases, and transferable licenses for their extraction. Continuation of these rights shall depend upon the performance of annual labor, or the payment of fees, rents, or royalties, or upon other requirements as may be pre scribed by law. Surface uses of land by a mineral claimant shall be limited to those necessary for the extraction or basic processing of the mineral deposits, or for both. Discovery and appropriation shall initiate a right, subject to further requirements of law, to patent of mineral lands if authorized by the State and not prohibited by Congress. The provisions of this section shall apply to all other minerals reserved to the State which by law are declared subject to appropriation.

Mineral Leases
and Permits

Section 12. The legislature shall provide for the issuance, types and terms of leases for coal, oil, gas, oil shale, sodium, phosphate, potash, sulfur, pumice, and other minerals as may be prescribed by law. Leases and permits giving the exclusive right of exploration for these minerals for specific periods and areas, subject to reasonable concurrent exploration as to different classes of minerals, may be authorized by law. Like leases and permits giving the exclusive right of prospecting by geophysical, geochemical, and similar methods for all minerals may also be authorized by law.

Water
Rights

Section 13. All surface and subsurface waters reserved
to the people for common use, except mineral and
medicinal waters, are subject to appropriation. Priority
of appropriation shall give prior right. Except for public
water supply, an appropriation of water shall be limited
to stated purposes and subject to preferences among
beneficial uses, concurrent or otherwise, as prescribed by
law, and to the general reservation of fish and wildlife.

Access to
Navigable
Waters

Section 14. Free access to the navigable or public
waters of the State, as defined by the legislature, shall
not be denied any citizen of the United States or
resident of the State, except that the legislature may
by general law regulate and limit such access for other
beneficial uses or public purposes.

No Exclussive
Right of Fishery

Section 15. No exclusive right or special privilege of
fishery shall be created or authorized in the natural
waters of the State. This section does not restrict the
power of the State to limit entry into any fishery
for purposes of resource conservation, to prevent
economic distress among fishermen and those
dependent upon them for a livelihood and to promote
the efficient development of aquaculture in the State.
[Amended 1972]

Protection of
Rights

Section 16. No person shall be involuntarily divested
of his right to the use of waters, his interests in lands,
or improvements affecting either, except for a superior
beneficial use or public purpose and then only with
just compensation and by operation of law.

Uniform
Application

Section 17. Laws and regulations governing the use or disposal of natural resources shall apply equally to all persons similarly situated with reference to the subject matter and purpose to be served by the law or regulation.

Private Ways
of Necessity

Section 18. Proceedings in eminent domain may be undertaken for private ways of necessity to permit essential access for extraction or utilization of resources. Just compensation shall be made for property taken or for resultant damages to other property rights.

Article IX
Finance and Taxation

Taxing Power

Section 1. The power of taxation shall never be surrendered. This power shall not be suspended or contracted away, except as provided in this article.

Non-discimination

Section 2. The lands and other property belonging to citizens of the United States residing without the State shall never be taxed at a higher rate than the lands and other property belonging to the residents of the State.

Assessment Standards

Section 3. Standards for appraisal of all property assessed by the State or its political subdivisions shall be prescribed by law.

Exemptions

Section 4. The real and personal property of the State or its political subdivisions shall be exempt from taxation under conditions and exceptions which may be provided by law. All, or any portion of, property used exclusively for non-profit religious, charitable, cemetery, or educational purposes, as de fined by law, shall be exempt from taxation. Other exemptions of like or different kind may be granted by general law. All valid existing exemptions shall be retained until otherwise provided by law.

Interests in Government Property

Section 5. Private leaseholds, contracts, or interests in land or property owned or held by the United States, the State, or its political subdivisions, shall be taxable to the extent of the interests.

Public Purpose

Section 6. No tax shall be levied, or appropriation of public money made, or public property transferred, nor shall the public credit be used, except for a public purpose.

Dedicated
Funds

Section 7. The proceeds of any state tax or license shall not be dedicated to any special purpose, except as provided in section 15 of this article or when required by the federal government for state participation in federal programs. This provision shall not prohibit the continuance of any dedication for special purposes existing upon the date of ratification of this section by the people of Alaska. [Amended 1976]

State Debt

Section 8. No state debt shall be contracted unless authorized by law for capital improvements or unless authorized by law for housing loans for veterans, and ratified by a majority of the qualified voters of the State who vote on the question. The State may, as provided by law and without ratification, contract debt for the purpose of repelling invasion, suppressing insurrection, defending the State in war, meeting natural disasters, or redeeming indebtedness outstanding at the time this constitution becomes effective. [Amended 1982]

Local Debts

Section 9. No debt shall be contracted by any political subdivision of the State, unless authorized for capital improvements by its governing body and ratified by a majority vote of those qualified to vote and voting on the question.

Interim
Borrowing

Section 10. The State and its political subdivisions may borrow money to meet appropriations for any fiscal year in anticipation of the collection of the revenues for that year, but all debt so contracted shall be paid before the end of the next fiscal year.

Exceptions

Section 11. The restrictions on contracting debt do not apply to debt incurred through the issuance of revenue bonds by a public enterprise or public corporation of the State or a political subdivision, when the only security is the revenues of the enterprise or corporation. The restrictions do not apply to indebtedness to be paid from special assessments on the benefited property, nor do they apply to refunding indebtedness of the State or its political subdivisions.

Budget

Section 12. The governor shall submit to the legislature, at a time fixed by law, a budget for the next fiscal year setting forth all proposed expenditures and anticipated income of all departments, offices, and agencies of the State. The governor, at the same time, shall submit a general appropriation bill to authorize the proposed expenditures, and a bill or bills covering recommendations in the budget for new or additional revenues.

Expenditures

Section 13. No money shall be withdrawn from the treasury except in accordance with appropriations made by law. No obligation for the payment of money shall be incurred except as authorized by law. Unobligated appropriations outstanding at the end of the period of time specified by law shall be void.

Legislative
Post-audit

Section 14. The legislature shall appoint an auditor to serve at its pleasure. He shall be a certified public accountant. The auditor shall conduct post-audits as prescribed by law and shall report to the legislature and to the governor.

Alaska
Permanent
Fund

Section 15. At least twenty-five percent of all mineral lease rentals, royalties, royalty sale proceeds, federal mineral revenue sharing payments and bonuses received by the State shall be placed in a permanent fund, the principal of which shall be used only for those income-producing investments specifically designated by law as eligible for permanent fund investments. All income from the permanent fund shall be deposited in the general fund unless otherwise provided by law. [Amended 1976]

Appropriation
Limit

Section 16. Except for appropriations for Alaska permanent fund dividends, appropriations of revenue bond proceeds, appropriations required to pay the principal and interest on general obligation bonds, and appropriations of money received from a non-State source in trust for a specific purpose, including revenues of a public enterprise or public corporation of the State that issues revenue bonds, appropriations from the treasury made for a fiscal year shall not exceed $2,500,000,000 by more than the cumulative change, derived from federal indices as prescribed by law, in population and inflation since July 1, 1981. Within this limit, at least one-third shall be reserved for capital projects and loan appropriations. The legislature may exceed this limit in bills for appropriations to the Alaska permanent fund and in bills for appropriations for capital projects, whether of bond proceeds or otherwise, if each bill is approved by the governor, or passed by affirmative vote of three-fourths of the membership of the legislature over a veto or item veto, or becomes law without signature, and is also approved by the voters as prescribed by law.

Appropriation
Limit
(cont.)

Each bill for appropriations for capital projects in excess of the limit shall be confined to capital projects of the same type, and the voters shall, as provided by law, be informed of the cost of operations and maintenance of the capital projects. No other appropriation in excess of this limit may be made except to meet a state of disaster declared by the governor as prescribed by law. The governor shall cause any unexpended and unappropriated balance to be invested so as to yield competitive market rates to the treasury. [Amended 1982]

Budget
Reserve
Fund

Section 17. (a) There is established as a separate fund in the State treasury the budget reserve fund. Except for money deposited into the permanent fund under section 15 of this article, all money received by the State after July 1, 1990, as a result of the termination, through settlement or otherwise, of an administrative proceeding or of litigation in a State or federal court involving mineral lease bonuses, rentals, royalties, royalty sale proceeds, federal mineral revenue sharing payments or bonuses, or involving taxes imposed on mineral income, production, or property, shall be deposited in the budget reserve fund. Money in the budget reserve fund shall be invested so as to yield competitive market rates to the fund. Income of the fund shall be retained in the fund. section 7 of this article does not apply to deposits made to the fund under this subsection. Money may be appropriated from the fund only as authorized under (b) or (c) of this section.

Budget
Reserve
Fund
(cont.)

(b) If the amount available for appropriation for a fiscal year is less than the amount appropriated for the previous fiscal year, an appropriation may be made from the budget reserve fund. However, the amount appropriated from the fund under this subsection may not exceed the amount necessary, when added to other funds available for appropriation, to provide for total appropriations equal to the amount of appropriations made in the previous calendar year for the previous fiscal year.

(c) An appropriation from the budget reserve fund may be made for any public purpose upon affirmative vote of three-fourths of the members of each house of the legislature.

(d) If an appropriation is made from the budget reserve fund, until the amount appropriated is repaid, the amount of money in the general fund available for appropriation at the end of each succeeding fiscal year shall be deposited in the budget reserve fund. The legislature shall implement this subsection by law. [Amended 1990]

Article X
Local Government

Purpose and
Construction

Section 1. The purpose of this article is to provide for maximum local self-government with a minimum of local government units, and to prevent duplication of tax-levying jurisdictions. A liberal construction shall be given to the powers of local government units.

Local
Government
Powers

Section 2. All local government powers shall be vested in boroughs and cities. The State may delegate taxing powers to organized boroughs and cities only.

Boroughs

Section 3. The entire State shall be divided into boroughs, organized or unorganized. They shall be established in a manner and according to standards provided by law. The standards shall include population, geography, economy, transportation, and other factors. Each borough shall embrace an area and population with common interests to the maxi mum degree possible. The legislature shall classify boroughs and prescribe their powers and functions. Methods by which boroughs may be organized, incorporated, merged, consolidated, reclassified, or dis solved shall be prescribed by law.

Assembly

Section 4. The governing body of the organized borough shall be the assembly, and its composition shall be established by law or charter. [Amended 1972]

Service Areas

Section 5. Service areas to provide special services within an organized borough may be established, altered, or abolished by the assembly, subject to the provisions of law or charter. A new service area shall not be established if, consistent with the purposes of this article, the new service can be provided by an existing service area, by incorporation as a city, or by annexation to a city. The assembly may authorize the levying of taxes, charges, or assessments within a service area to finance the special services.

Unorganized Boroughs

Section 6. The legislature shall provide for the performance of services it deems necessary or advisable in unorganized boroughs, allowing for maximum local participation and responsibility. It may exercise any power or function in an unorganized borough which the assembly may exercise in an organized borough.

Cities

Section 7. Cities shall be incorporated in a manner prescribed by law, and shall be a part of the borough in which they are located. Cities shall have the powers and functions conferred by law or charter. They may be merged, consolidated, classified, reclassified, or dissolved in the manner provided by law.

Council

Section 8. The governing body of a city shall be the council.

Charters

Section 9. The qualified voters of any borough of the first class or city of the first class may adopt, amend, or repeal a home rule charter in a manner provided by law. In the absence of such legislation, the governing body of a borough or city of the first class shall provide the procedure for the preparation and adoption or rejection of the charter. All charters, or parts or amendments of charters, shall be submitted to the qualified voters of the borough or city, and shall become effective if approved by a majority of those who vote on the specific question.

Extended
Home Rule

Section 10. The legislature may extend home rule to other boroughs and cities.

Home Rule
Powers

Section 11. A home rule borough or city may exercise all legislative powers not prohibited by law or by charter.

Boundaries

Section 12. A local boundary commission or board shall be established by law in the executive branch of the state government. The commission or board may consider any proposed local government boundary change. It may present proposed changes to the legislature during the first ten days of any regular session. The change shall become effective forty-five days after presentation or at the end of the session, whichever is earlier, unless disapproved by a resolution concurred in by a majority of the members of each house. The commission or board, subject to law, may establish procedures whereby boundaries may be adjusted by local action.

Agreements;
Transfer of
Powers

Section 13. Agreements, including those for cooperative or joint administration of any functions or powers, may be made by any local government with any other local government, with the State, or with the United States, unless otherwise provided by law or charter. A city may transfer to the borough in which it is located any of its powers or functions unless prohibited by law or charter, and may in like manner revoke the transfer.

Local
Government
Agency

Section 14. An agency shall be established by law in the executive branch of the state government to advise and assist local governments. It shall review their activities, collect and publish local government information, and perform other duties prescribed by law.

Special
Service
Districts

Section 15. Special service districts existing at the time a borough is organized shall be integrated with the government of the borough as provided by law.

ARTICLE XI
INITIATIVE, REFERENDUM, AND RECALL

Initiative and Referendum

Section 1. The people may propose and enact laws by the initiative, and approve or reject acts of the legislature by the referendum.

Application

Section 2. An initiative or referendum is proposed by an application containing the bill to be initiated or the act to be referred. The application shall be signed by not less than one hundred qualified voters as sponsors, and shall be filed with the lieutenant governor. If he finds it in proper form he shall so certify. Denial of certification shall be subject to judicial review. [Amended 1970]

Petition

Section 3. After certification of the application, a petition containing a summary of the subject matter shall be prepared by the lieutenant governor for circulation by the sponsors. If signed by qualified voters who are equal in number to at least ten percent of those who voted in the preceding general election, who are resident in at least three-fourths of the house districts of the State, and who, in each of those house districts, are equal in number to at least seven percent of those who voted in the preceding general election in the house district, it may be filed with the lieutenant governor. [Amended 1970, 1998 & 2004]

Initiative Election

Section 4. An initiative petition may be filed at any time. The lieutenant governor shall prepare a ballot title and proposition summarizing the proposed law, and shall place them on the ballot for the first statewide election held more than one hundred twenty days after adjournment of the legislative session following the filing. If, before the election, substantially the same measure has been enacted, the petition is void. [Amended 1970]

Referendum
Election

Section 5. If a majority of the votes cast on the proposition favor its adoption, the initiated measure is enacted. If a majority of the votes cast on the proposition favor the rejection of an act referred, it is rejected. The lieutenant governor shall certify the election returns. An initiated law becomes effective ninety days after certification, is not subject to veto, and may not be repealed by the legislature within two years of its effective date. It may be amended at any time. An act rejected by referendum is void thirty days after certification. Additional procedures for the initiative and referendum may be prescribed by law. [Amended 1970]

Enactment

Section 6. If a majority of the votes cast on the proposition favor its adoption, the initiated measure is enacted. If a majority of the votes cast on the proposition favor the rejection of an act referred, it is rejected. The secretary of state shall certify the election returns. An initiated law becomes effective ninety days after certification, is not subject to veto, and may not be repealed by the legislature within two years of its effective date. It may be amended at any time. An act rejected by referendum is void thirty days after certification. Additional procedures for the initiative and referendum may be prescribed by law.

Restrictions

Section 7. The initiative shall not be used to dedicate revenues, make or repeal appropriations, create courts, define the jurisdiction of courts or pre scribe their rules, or enact local or special legislation. The referendum shall not be applied to dedications of revenue, to appropriations, to local or special legislation, or to laws necessary for the immediate preservation of the public peace, health, or safety.

Recall

Section 8. All elected public officials in the State, except judicial officers, are subject to recall by the voters of the State or political subdivision from which elected. Procedures and grounds for recall shall be prescribed by the legislature.

Article XII
General Provisions

State
Boundaries

Section 1. The State of Alaska shall consist of all the territory, together with the territorial waters appurtenant thereto, included in the Territory of Alaska upon the date of ratification of this constitution by the people of Alaska.

Intergovern-
mental
Relations

Section 2. The State and its political subdivisions may cooperate with the United States and its territories, and with other states and their political subdivisions on matters of common interest. The respective legislative bodies may make appropriations for this purpose.

Office of
Profit

Section 3. Service in the armed forces of the United States or of the State is not an office or position of profit as the term is used in this constitution.

Disqualification
for Disloyalty

Section 4. No person who advocates, or who aids or belongs to any party or organization or association which advocates, the overthrow by force or violence of the government of the United States or of the State shall be qualified to hold any public office of trust or profit under this constitution.

Oath of
Office

Section 5. All public officers, before entering upon the duties of their offices, shall take and subscribe to the following oath or affirmation: "I do solemnly swear (or affirm) that I will support and de fend the Constitution of the United States and the Constitution of the State of Alaska, and that I will faithfully discharge my duties as ______________ to the best of my ability." The legislature may prescribe further oaths or affirmations.

Merit System **Section 6.** The legislature shall establish a system under which the merit principle will govern the employment of persons by the State.

Retirement Systems **Section 7.** Membership in employee retirement systems of the State or its political subdivisions shall constitute a contractual relationship. Accrued benefits of these systems shall not be diminished or impaired.

Residual Power **Section 8.** The enumeration of specified powers in this constitution shall not be construed as limiting the powers of the State.

Provisions Self-executing **Section 9.** The provisions of this constitution shall be construed to be self-executing whenever possible.

Interpretation **Section 10.** Titles and subtitles shall not be used in construing this constitution. Personal pronouns used in this constitution shall be construed as including either sex.

Law-making Power **Section 11.** As used in this constitution, the terms "by law" and "by the legislature," or variations of these terms, are used interchangeably when related to law-making powers. Unless clearly inapplicable, the law-making powers assigned to the legislature may be exercised by the people through the initiative, subject to the limitations of Article XI.

Disclaimer and
Agreement

Section 12. The State of Alaska and its people forever disclaim all right and title in or to any property belonging to the United States, or subject to its disposition, and not granted or confirmed to the State or its political subdivisions, by or under the act admitting Alaska to the Union. The State and its people further disclaim all right or title in or to any property, including fishing rights, the right or title to which may be held by or for any Indian, Eskimo, or Aleut, or community thereof, as that right or title is defined in the act of admission. The State and its people agree that, unless otherwise provided by Congress, the property, as described in this section, shall remain subject to the absolute disposition of the United States. They further agree that no taxes will be imposed upon any such property, until otherwise provided by the Congress. This tax exemption shall not apply to property held by individuals in fee without restrictions on alienation.

Consetnt to
Act of
Admimssion

Section 13. All provisions of the act admitting Alaska to the Union which reserve rights or powers to the United States, as well as those prescribing the terms or conditions of the grants of lands or other property, are consented to fully by the State and its people.

Approval of
Federal
Amendment
to Statehood
Act Affecting
an Interest of
the State under
that Act

Section 14. A federal statute or proposed federal
statute that affects an interest of this State under the
Act admitting Alaska to the Union is ineffective as
against the State interest unless approved by a two-
thirds vote of each house of the legislature or approved
by the people of the State. The legislature may, by a
resolution passed by a majority vote of each house,
place the question of approval of the federal statute
on the ballot for the next general election unless in
the resolution placing the question of approval, the
legislature requires the question to be placed before
the voters at a special election. The approval of
the federal statute by the people of the State is not
effective unless the federal statute described in the
resolution is ratified by a majority of the qualified
voters of the State who vote on the question. Unless a
summary of the question is provided in the resolution
passed by the legislature, the lieutenant governor shall
prepare an impartial summary of the question. The
lieutenant governor shall present the question to the
voters so that a "yes" vote on the question is a vote to
approve the federal statute. [Amended 1996]

Article XIII
Amendment and Revision

Amendments

Section 1. Amendments to this constitution may be proposed by a two-thirds vote of each house of the legislature. The lieutenant governor shall prepare a ballot title and proposition summarizing each proposed amendment, and shall place them on the ballot for the next general election. If a majority of the votes cast on the proposition favor the amendment, it shall be adopted. Unless otherwise provided in the amendment, it becomes effective thirty days after the certification of the election returns by the lieutenant governor. [Amended 1970, 1974]

Convention

Section 2. The legislature may call constitutional conventions at any time.

Call by
Referendum

Section 3. If during any ten-year period a
constitutional convention has not been held, the
lieutenant governor shall place on the ballot for the
next general election the question: "Shall there be a
Constitutional Convention?" If a majority of the votes
cast on the question are in the negative, the question
need not be placed on the ballot until the end of the
next ten-year period. If a majority of the votes cast
on the question are in the affirmative, delegates to
the convention shall be chosen at the next regular
statewide election, unless the legislature provides
for the election of the delegates at a special election.
The lieutenant governor shall issue the call for the
convention. Unless other provisions have been made
by law, the call shall conform as nearly as possible to
the act calling the Alaska Constitutional Convention
of 1955, including, but not limited to, number
of members, districts, election and certification of
delegates, and submission and ratification of revisions
and ordinances. The appropriation provisions of the
call shall be self-executing and shall constitute a first
claim on the state treasury. [Amended 1970]

Powers

Section 4. Constitutional conventions shall have
plenary power to amend or revise the constitution,
subject only to ratification by the people. No call for
a constitutional convention shall limit these powers of
the convention.

ARTICLE XV
SCHEDULE OF TRANSITIONAL MEASURES

To provide an orderly transition from a territorial to a state form of government, it is declared and ordained:

Continuance of Laws

Section 1. All laws in force in the Territory of Alaska on the effective date of this constitution and consistent therewith shall continue in force until they expire by their own limitation, are amended, or repealed.

Saving of Existing Rights and Liabilities

Section 2. Except as otherwise provided in this constitution, all rights, titles, actions, suits, contracts, and liabilities and all civil, criminal, or administrative proceedings shall continue unaffected by the change from territorial to state government, and the State shall be the legal successor to the Territory in these matters.

Local Government

Section 3. Cities, school districts health districts, public utility districts, and other local subdivisions of government existing on the effective date of this constitution shall continue to exercise their powers and functions under existing law, pending enactment of legislation to carry out the provisions of this constitution. New local subdivisions of government shall be created only in accordance with this constitution.

Continuance of Office

Section 4. All officers of the Territory, or under its laws, on the effective date of this constitution shall continue to perform the duties of their offices in a manner consistent with this constitution until they are superseded by officers of the State.

Corresponding Qualifications

Section 5. Residence, citizenship, or other qualifications under the Territory may be used toward the fulfillment of corresponding qualifications required by this constitution.

Governor to
Proclaim
Election

Section 6. When the people of the Territory ratify this constitution and it is approved by the duly constituted authority of the United States, the governor of the Territory shall, within thirty days after receipt of the official notification of such approval, issue a proclamation and take necessary measures to hold primary and general elections for all state elective offices provided for by this constitution.

First State
Elections

Section 7. The primary election shall take place not less than forty nor more than ninety days after the proclamation by the governor of the Territory. The general election shall take place not less than ninety days after the primary election. The elections shall be governed by this constitution and by applicable territorial laws.

United States
Senators and
Representative

Section 8. The officers to be elected at the first general election shall include two senators and one representative to serve in the Congress of the United States, unless senators and a representative have been previously elected and seated. One senator shall be elected for the long term and one senator for the short term, each term to expire on the third day of January in an odd-numbered year to be determined by authority of the United States. The term of the representative shall expire on the third day of January in the odd-numbered year immediately following his assuming office. If the first representative is elected in an even-numbered year to take office in that year, a representative shall be elected at the same time to fill the full term commencing on the third day of January of the following year, and the same person may be elected for both terms.

Terms of First Governor and Lieutenant Governor

Section 9. The First Governor and Lieutenant Governor shall hold office for a term beginning with the day on which they assume office and ending at noon on the first Monday in December of the even-numbered year following the next presidential election. This term shall count as a full term for purposes of determining eligibility for re-election only if it is four years or more in duration. [Amended 1970]

Election of First Senators

Section 10. At the first state general election, one senator shall be chosen for a two-year term from each of the following senate districts, described in Section 2 of Article XIV: A, B, D, E, G, I, J, L, N, and O. At the same election, one senator shall be chosen for a four-year term from each of the following senate districts, described in Section 2 of Article XIV: A, C, E, F, H, J, K, M, N, and P.

Terms of First State Legislators

Section 11. The first state legislators shall hold office for a term beginning with the day on which they assume office and ending at noon on the fourth Monday in January after the next general election, except that senators elected for four-year terms shall serve an additional two years thereafter. If the first general election is held in an even-numbered year, it shall be deemed to be the general election for that year.

Election Returns

Section 12. The returns of the first general election shall be made, canvassed, and certified in the manner prescribed by law. The governor of the Territory shall certify the results to the President of the United States.

Assumption
of Office

Section 13. When the President of the United States issues a proclamation announcing the results of the election, and the State has been admitted into the Union, the officers elected and qualified shall assume office.

First Session
of Legislature

Section 14. The governor shall call a special session of the first state legislature within thirty days after the presidential proclamation unless a regular session of the legislature falls within that period. The special session shall not be limited as to duration.

First Legislators:
Office Holding

Section 15. The provisions of Section 5 of Article II shall not prohibit any member of the first state legislature from holding any office or position created during his first term.

First Judicial
Council

Section 16. The first members of the judicial council shall, notwithstanding Section 8 of Article IV, be appointed for terms as follows: three attorney members for one, three, and five years respectively, and three non-attorney members for two, four, and six years respectively. The six members so appointed shall, in accordance with Section 5 of Article IV, submit to the governor nominations to fill the initial vacancies on the superior court and the supreme court, including the office of chief justice. After the initial vacancies on the superior and supreme courts are filled, the chief justice shall assume his seat on the judicial council.

Transfer
of Court
Jurisdiction

Section 17. Until the courts provided for in Article IV are organized, the courts, their jurisdiction, and the judicial system shall remain as constituted on the date of admission unless otherwise provided by law. When the state courts are organized, new actions shall be commenced and filed therein, and all causes, other than those under the jurisdiction of the United States, pending in the courts existing on the date of admission, shall be transferred to the proper state court as though commenced, filed, or lodged in those courts in the first instance, except as otherwise provided by law.

Territorial
Assets and
Liabilities

Section 18. The debts and liabilities of the Territory of Alaska shall be assumed and paid by the State, and debts owed to the Territory shall be collected by the State. Assets and records of the Territory shall become the property of the State.

First Re-
apportionment

Section 19. The first reapportionment of the house of representatives shall be made immediately following the official reporting of the 1960 decennial census, or after the first regular legislative session if the session occurs thereafter, notwithstanding the provision as to time contained in Section 3 of Article VI. All other provisions of Article VI shall apply in the first reapportionment.

State Capital

Section 20. The capital of the State of Alaska shall be at Juneau.

Seal

Section 21. The seal of the Territory, substituting the word "State" for "Territory," shall be the seal of the State.

Flag

Section 22. The flag of the Territory shall be the flag of the State.

Special Voting Provision

Section 23. Citizens who legally voted in the general election of November 4, 1924, and who meet the residence requirements for voting, shall be entitled to vote notwithstanding the provisions of Section 1 of Article V.

Ordinances

Section 24. Ordinance No. 1 on ratification of the constitution, Ordinance No. 2 on the Alaska-Tennessee Plan, and Ordinance No. 3 on the abolition of fish traps, adopted by the Alaska Constitutional Convention and appended to this constitution shall be submitted to the voters and if ratified shall become effective as provided in each ordinance.

Effective Date

Section 25. This constitution shall take effect immediately upon the admission of Alaska into the Union as a state.

Appropriations for Relocation of the Capital

Section 26. If a majority of those voting on the question at the general election in 1982 approve the ballot proposition for the total cost to the State of providing for relocation of the capital, no additional voter approval of appropriations for that purpose within the cost approved by the voters is required under the 1982 amendment limiting increases in appropriations (art. IX, sec. 16). [Amended 1982]

Reconsideration of Amendment Limiting Increases in Appropriations

Section 27. If the 1982 amendment limiting appropriation increases (art. IX, sec. 16) is adopted, the lieutenant governor shall cause the ballot title and proposition for the amendment to be placed on the ballot again at the general election in 1986. If the majority of those voting on the proposition in 1986 rejects the amendment, it shall be repealed. [Amended 1982]

Application of Amendment

Section 28. The 1982 amendment limiting appropriation increases (art. IX, sec. 16) applies to appropriations made for fiscal year 1984 and thereafter. [Amended 1982]

Applicability of Amendments Providing for Redistricting of the Legislature

Section 29. The 1998 amendments relating to redistricting of the legislature (art. VI and art. XIV) apply only to plans for redistricting and proclamations of redistricting adopted on or after January 1, 2001. [Amended 1998]

Agreed upon by the delegates in Constitutional Convention assembled at the University of Alaska, this fifth day of February, in the year of our Lord one thousand nine hundred and fifty-six, and of the Independence of the United States the one hundred and eightieth.

R. ROLLAND ARMSTRONG
DOROTHY J. AWES
FRANK BARR
JOHN C. BOSWELL
SEABORN J. BUCKALEW, JR.
JOHN B. COGHILL
E. B. COLLINS
GEORGE D. COOPER
JOHN M. CROSS
EDWARD V. DAVIS
JAMES P. DOOGAN
TRUMAN C. EMBERG
WM. A. EGAN President of the Convention
HELEN FISCHER
VICTOR FISCHER
DOUGLAS GRAY
THOMAS C. HARRIS
JOHN S. HELLENTHAL
MILDRED R. HERMANN
HERB HILSCHER
JACK HINCKEL
JAMES HURLEY

MAURICE T. JOHNSON

YULE F. KILCHER

LEONARD H. KING

WILLIAM W. KNIGHT

PETER L. READER

W. W. LAWS

BURKE RILEY

ELDOR R. LEE

RALPH J. RIVERS

MAYNARD D. LONDBORG

VICTOR C. RIVERS

STEVE McCUTCHEON

JOHN H. ROSSWOG

GEORGE M. McLAUGHLIN

B. D. STEWART

ROBERT J. McNEALY

W. O. SMITH

JOHN A. McNEES

GEORGE SUNDBORG

M. R. MARSTON

DORA M. SWEENEY

IRWIN L. METCALF

WARREN A. TAYLOR

LESLIE NERLAND

H. R. VANDERLEEST

JAMES NOLAN

M. J. WALSH

KATHERINE D. NORDALE

BARRIE M. WHITE

FRANK PERATROVICH

ADA B. WIEN

CHRIS POULSEN

ATTEST: THOMAS B. STEWART Secretary of the Convention

THE ORDINANCES

Ordinance No. 1
Ratification of Constitution

Election

Section 1. The Constitution for the State of Alaska agreed upon by the delegates to the Alaska Constitutional Convention on February 5, 1956, shall be submitted to the voters of Alaska for ratification or rejection at the territorial primary election to be held on April 24, 1956. The election shall be conducted according to existing laws regulating primary elections so far as applicable.

Ballot

Section 2. Each elector who offers to vote upon this constitution shall be given a ballot by the election judges which will be separate from the ballot on which candidates in the primary election are listed. Each of the propositions offered by the Alaska Constitutional Convention shall be set forth separately, but on the same ballot form. The first proposition shall be as follows:

"Shall the Constitution for the State of Alaska prepared and agreed upon by the Alaska Constitutional Convention be adopted?"

☐   Yes
☐   No

Canvass

Section 3. The returns of this election shall be made to the governor of the Territory of Alaska, and shall be canvassed in substantially the manner provided by law for territorial elections.

Acceptance
and Approval

Section 4. If a majority of the votes cast on the proposition favor the constitution, then the constitution shall be deemed to be ratified by the people of Alaska to become effective as provided in the constitution.

Submission of
Constitution

Section 5. Upon ratification of the constitution, the governor of the Territory shall forthwith transmit a certified copy of the constitution to the President of the United States for submission to the Congress, together with a statement of the votes cast for and against ratification.

Ordinance No. 2
Alaska-Tennessee Plan

Statement
of Purpose

Section 1. The election of senators and a representative to serve in the Congress of the United States being necessary and proper to prepare for the ad mission of Alaska as a state of the Union, the following sections are hereby ordained, pursuant to Chapter 46, SLA 1955.

Ballot

Section 2. Each elector who offers to vote upon the ratification of the constitution may, upon the same ballot, vote on a second proposition, which shall be as follows:

"Shall Ordinance Number Two (Alaska-Tennessee Plan) of the Alaska Constitutional Convention, calling for the immediate election of two United States Senators and one United States Representative, be adopted?"

☐   Yes
☐   No

Approval

Section 3. Upon ratification of the constitution by the people of Alaska and separate approval of this ordinance by a majority of all votes cast for and against it, the remainder of this ordinance shall become effective.

Election of Senators and Representative

Section 4. Two United States senators and one United States representative shall be chosen at the 1956 general election.

Terms

Section 5. One senator shall be chosen for the regular term expiring on January 3, 1963, and the other for an initial short term expiring on January 3, 1961, unless when they are seated the Senate prescribes other expiration dates. The representative shall be chosen for the regular term of two years expiring January 3, 1959.

Qualification

Section 6. Candidates for senators and representative shall have the qualifications prescribed in the Constitution of the United States and shall be qualified voters of Alaska.

Other Office Holding

Section 7. Until the admission of Alaska as a state, the senators and representative may also hold or be nominated and elected to other offices of the United States or of the Territory of Alaska, provided that no person may receive compensation for more than one office.

Election Procedure

Section 8. Except as provided herein, the laws of the Territory governing elections to the office of Delegate to Congress shall, to the extent applicable, govern the election of the senators and representative. Territorial and other officials shall perform their duties with reference to this election accordingly.

Independent
Candidates

Section 9. Persons not representing any political party may become independent candidates for the offices of senator or representative by filing applications in the manner provided in Section 38-5-10, ACLA 1949, insofar as applicable. Applications must be filed in the office of the director of finance of the Territory on or before June 30, 1956.

Party
Nominations

Section 10. Party nominations for senators and representative shall, for this election only, be made by party conventions in the manner prescribed in Section 38-4-11, ACLA 1949, for filling a vacancy in a party nomination occurring after a primary election. The names of the candidates nominated shall be certified by the chairman and secretary of the central committee of each political party to the director of finance of the Territory on or before June 30, 1956.

Certification

Section 11. The director of finance shall certify the names of all candidates for senators and representative to the clerks of court by July 15, 1956. The clerks of court shall cause the names to be printed on the official ballot for the general election. In dependent candidates shall be identified as provided in Section 38-5-10, ACLA 1949. Candidates nominated at party conventions shall be identified with appropriate party designations as is provided by law for nominations at primary elections.

Ballot Form;
Who Elected

Section 12. The ballot form shall group separately the candidates seeking the regular senate term, those seeking the short senate term, and candidates for representative. The candidate for each office receiving the largest number of votes cast for that office shall be elected.

Duties and Emoluments

Section 13. The duties and emoluments of the offices of senator and representative shall be as prescribed by law.

Convention Assistance

Section 14. The president of the Alaska Constitutional Convention, or a person designated by him, may assist in carrying out the purposes of this ordinance. The unexpended and unobligated funds appropriated to the Alaska Constitutional Convention by Chapter 46, SLA 1955, may be used to defray expenses attributable to the referendum and the election required by this ordinance.

Alternate Effective Dates

Section 15. If the Congress of the United States seats the senators and representative elected pursuant to this ordinance and approves the constitution before the first election of state officers, then Section 25 of Article XV shall be void and shall be replaced by the following:

> "The provisions of the constitution applicable to the first election of state officers shall take effect immediately upon the admission of Alaska into the Union as a state. The remainder of the constitution shall take effect when the elected governor takes office."

Ordinance No. 3
Abolition of Fish Traps

Ballot

Section 1. Each elector who offers to vote upon the ratification of the constitution may, upon the same ballot, vote on a third proposition, which shall be as follows:

"Shall Ordinance Number Three of the Alaska Constitutional Convention, prohibiting the use of fish traps for the taking of salmon for commercial purposes in the coastal waters of the State, be adopted?"

☐ Yes
☐ No

Effect of
Referendum

Section 2. If the constitution shall be adopted by the electors and if a majority of all the votes cast for and against this ordinance favor its adoption, then the following shall become operative upon the effective date of the constitution:

"As a matter of immediate public necessity, to relieve economic distress among individual fishermen and those dependent upon them for a livelihood, to conserve the rapidly dwindling sup ply of salmon in Alaska, to insure fair competition among those engaged in commercial fishing, and to make manifest the will of the people of Alaska, the use of fish traps for the taking of salmon for commercial purposes is hereby prohibited in all the coastal waters of the State."